45 BY #45

45 BY #45

Trump's Presidency Summarized by His Most Epic Tweets

EVA M. PARONYAN

VivaFullife LLC

I envisioned this book and began compiling tweets during Trump's first year in office, but was really called to bring it to life when the Twitter ban occurred. Additional content was sourced from https://www.thetrumparchive.com/. Thanks to Brendan Brown for his tremendous work in creating this public resource!

Please note that Twitter is not affiliated with this book in any way, and Twitter's guidelines were followed in sharing this public domain content.

Illustrations were inspired either by photography or video screenshots. Appropriate credit is given per available source information.

Finally, thank you to everyone who supported this project - you know who you are!

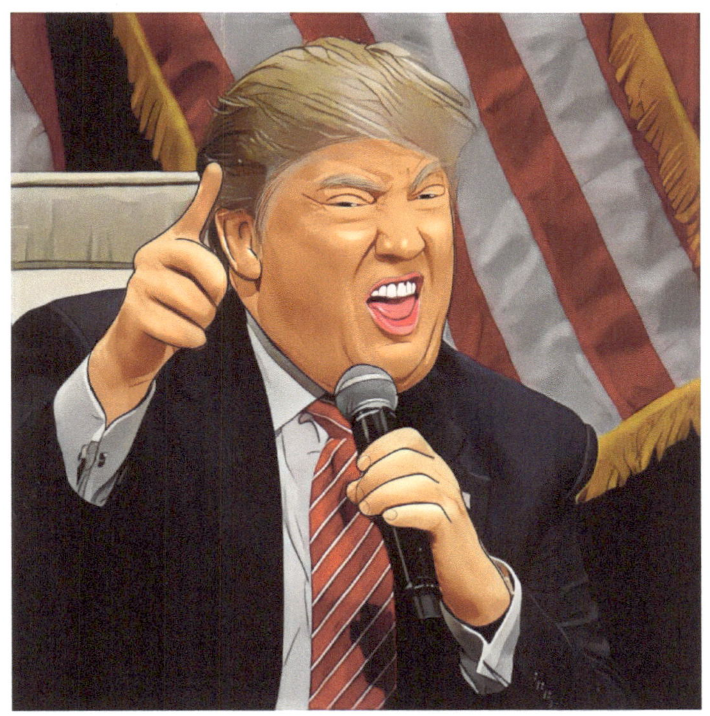

Inspired by Chris Keane/Reuters photo

Jan 20th 2017 - 12:54:36 PM EST

We will bring back our jobs. We will bring back our borders. We will bring back our wealth - and we will bring back our dreams!

Jan 24th 2017 - 9:16:19 PM EST

Congratulations to @FoxNews for being number one in inauguration ratings. They were many times higher than FAKE NEWS @CNN - public is smart!

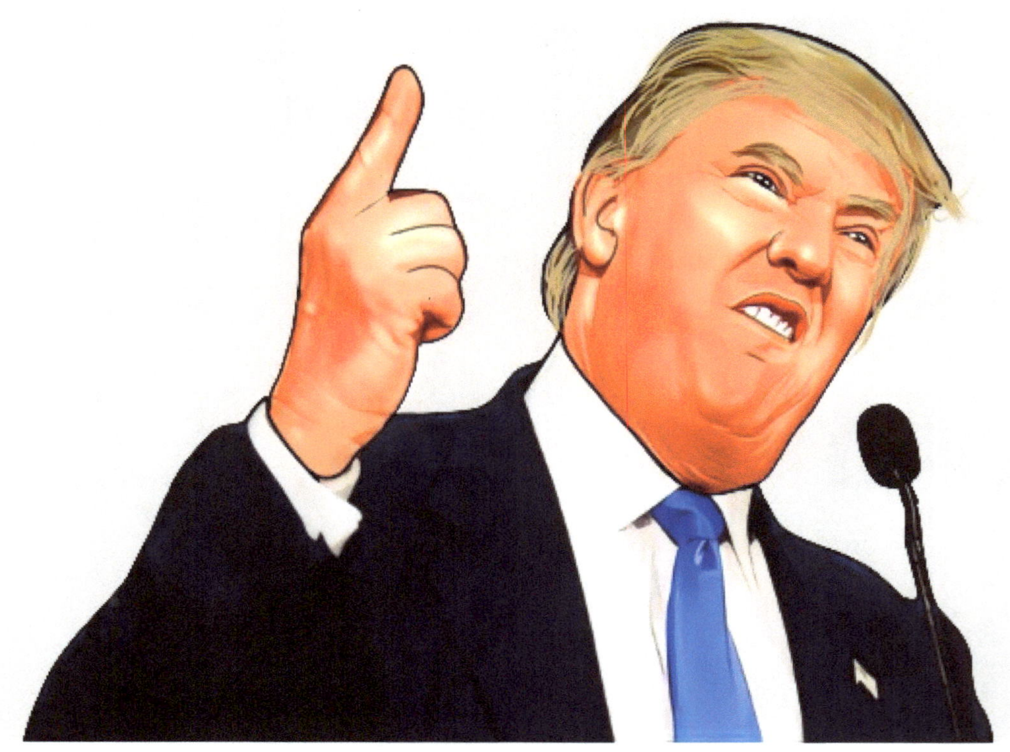

Inspired by Dominick Reuter/Reuters photo

Feb 3rd 2017 - 6:08:38 PM EST

We must keep "evil" out of our country!

Mar 14th 2017 - 12:12:22 PM EST

Great optimism in America – and the results will be even better! https://t.co/SYBl47CsZn

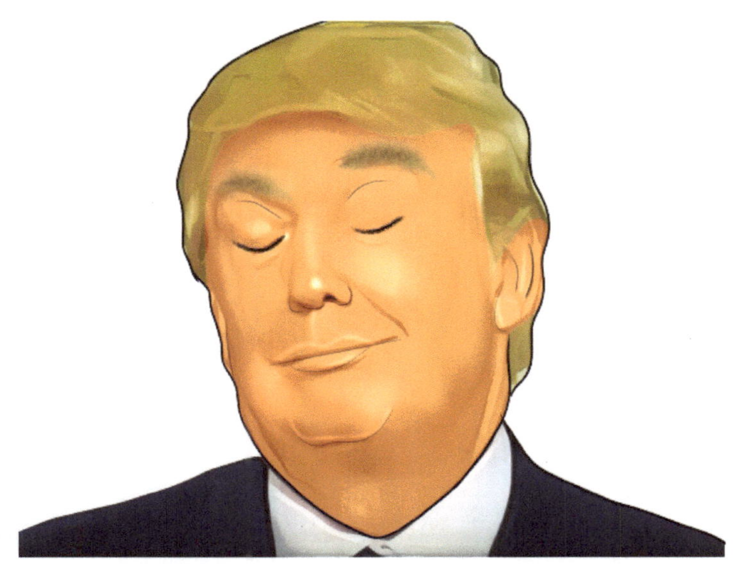

Inspired by screenshot of https://www.cnn.com/videos/tv/2015/12/17/faces-of-donald-trump-sequel-moos-dnt-erin.cnn

May 31st 2017 - 12:06:25 AM EST
Deleted

Despite the constant negative press covfefe

May 31st 2017 - 6:09:22 AM EST

Who can figure out the true meaning of "covfefe" ??? Enjoy!

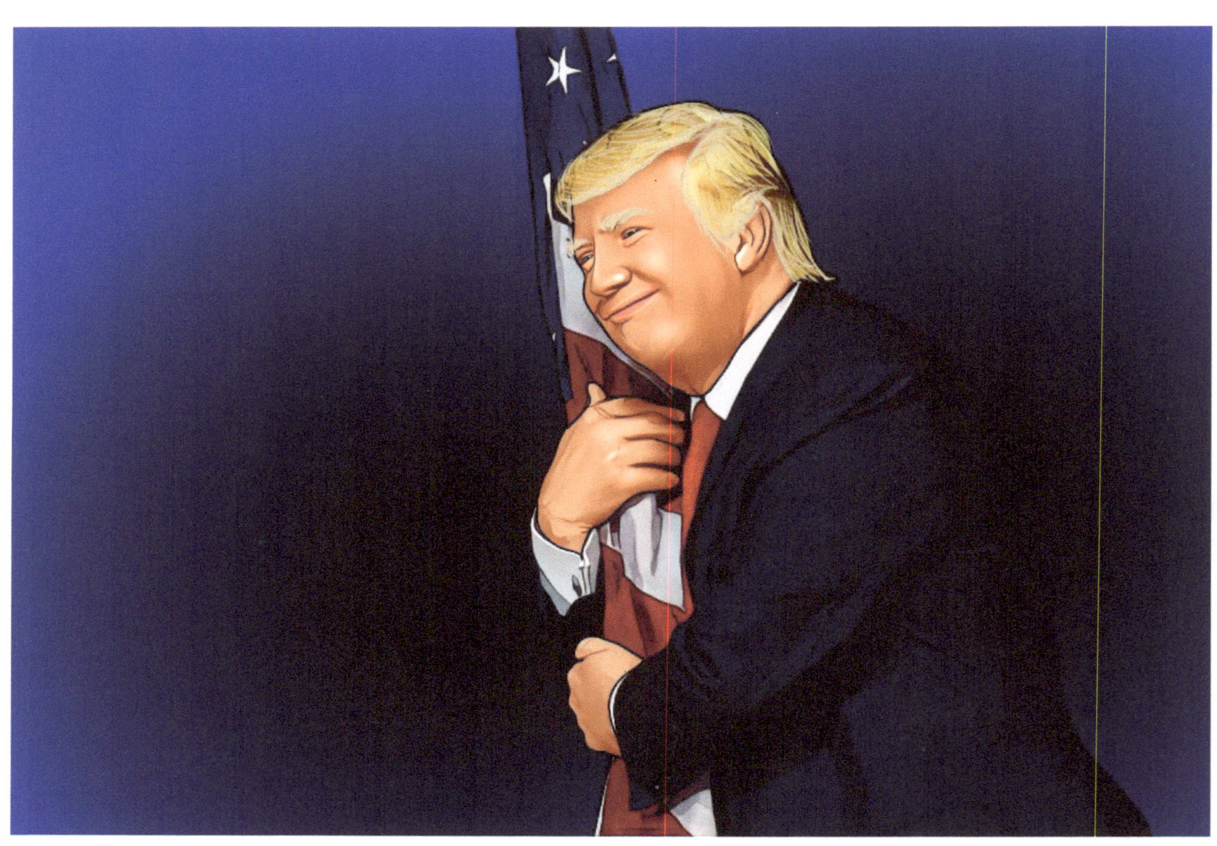

Inspired by Jonathan Ernst/Reuters photo

Jul 1st 2017 - 6:41:58 PM EST

My use of social media is not Presidential - it's MODERN DAY PRESIDENTIAL. Make America Great Again!

Aug 12th 2017 - 1:19:13 PM EST

We ALL must be united & condemn all that hate stands for. There is no place for this kind of violence in America. Lets come together as one!

Sep 23rd 2017 - 8:45:19 AM EST

Going to the White House is considered a great honor for a championship team.Stephen Curry is hesitating,therefore invitation is withdrawn!

Sep 24th 2017 - 6:44:52 AM EST

If NFL fans refuse to go to games until players stop disrespecting our Flag & Country, you will see change take place fast. Fire or suspend!

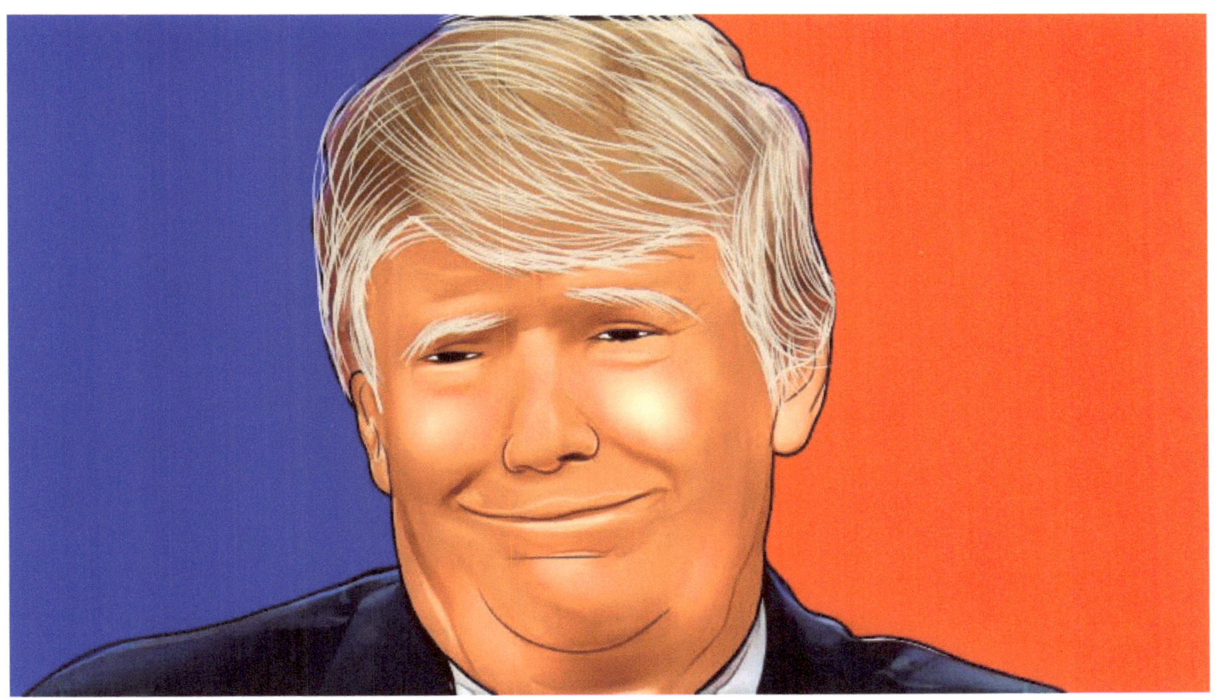

Inspired by Robyn Beck/AFP/Getty Images photo

Nov 11th 2017 - 7:48:01 PM EST

"Why would Kim Jong-un insult me by calling me ""old,"" when I would NEVER call him ""short and fat?""
Oh well, I try so hard to be his friend -

and maybe someday that will happen!"

Dec 24th 2017 - 9:56:19 PM EST

People are proud to be saying Merry Christmas again. I am proud to have led the charge against the assault of our cherished and beautiful phrase.

MERRY CHRISTMAS!!!!!

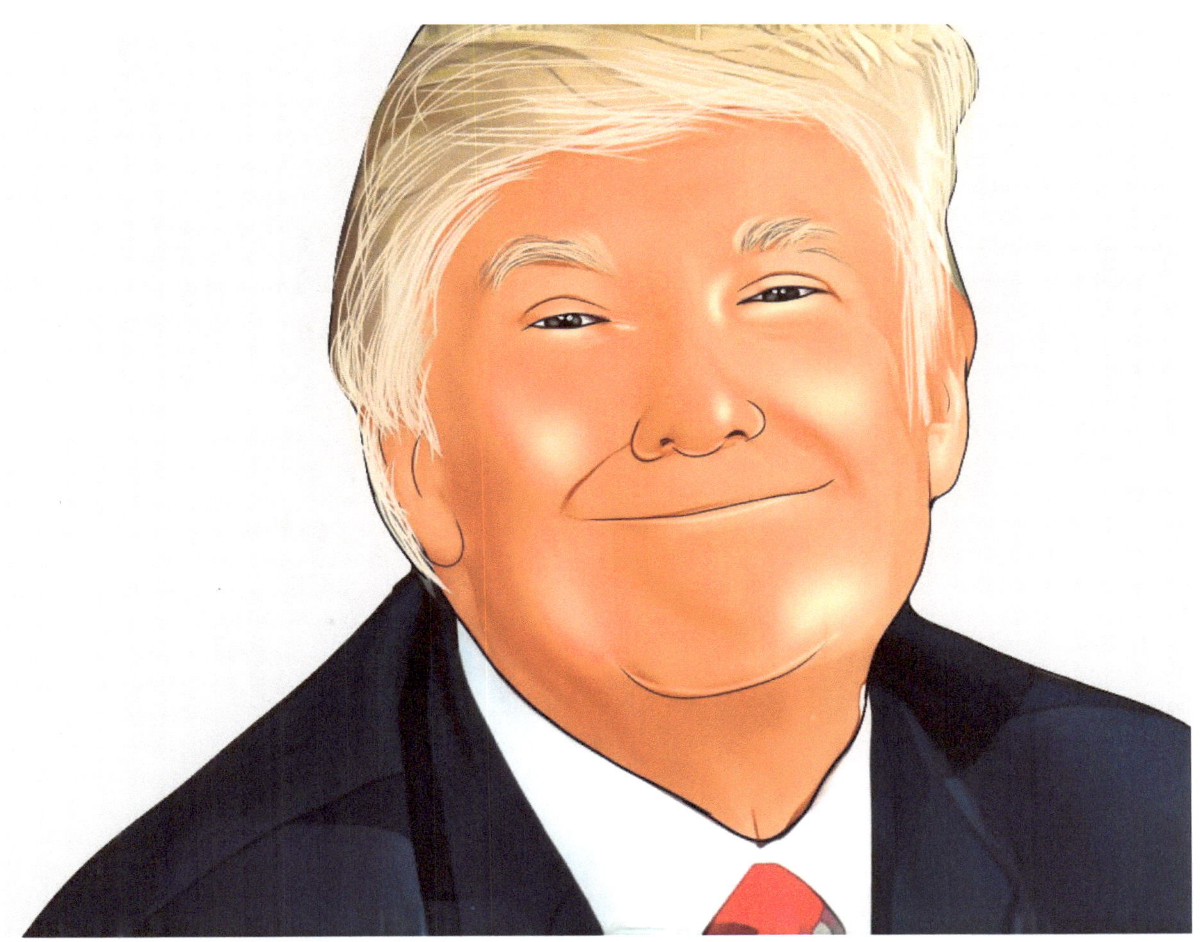

Inspired by Mark Wilson/Getty Images photo

Jan 2nd 2018 - 7:49:19 PM EST

North Korean Leader Kim Jong Un just stated that the "Nuclear Button is on his desk at all times." Will someone from his depleted and food starved regime please inform him that I too have a Nuclear Button, but it is a much bigger &, more powerful one than his, and my Button works!

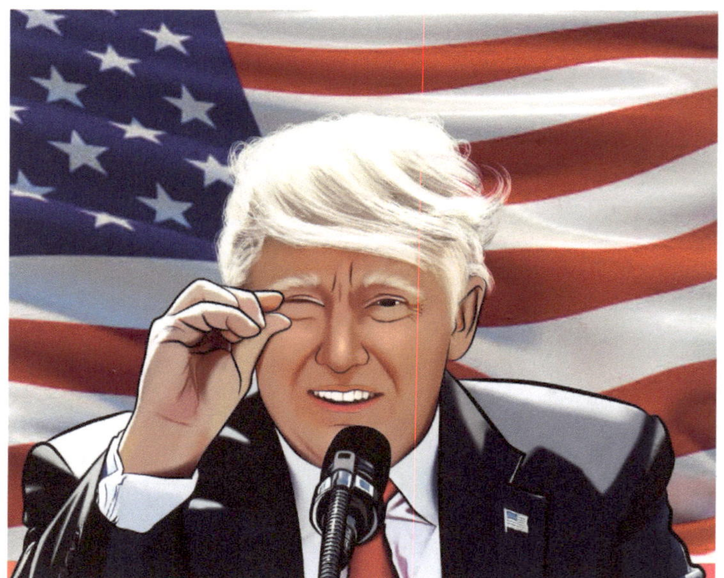

Inspired by Kevin Lamarque/Reuters/Newscom photo

Mar 2nd 2018 - 6:07:40 AM EST

Alec Baldwin, whose dying mediocre career was saved by his terrible impersonation of me on SNL, now says playing me was agony. Alec, it was agony for those who were forced to watch. Bring back Darrell Hammond, funnier and a far greater talent!

Mar 22nd 2018 - 6:19:57 AM EST

Crazy Joe Biden is trying to act like a tough guy. Actually, he is weak, both mentally and physically, and yet he threatens me, for the second time, with physical assault. He doesn't know me, but he would go down fast and hard, crying all the way. Don't threaten people Joe!

Apr 15th 2018 - 8:32:16 AM EST

I never asked Comey for Personal Loyalty. I hardly even knew this guy. Just another of his many lies. His "memos" are self serving and FAKE!

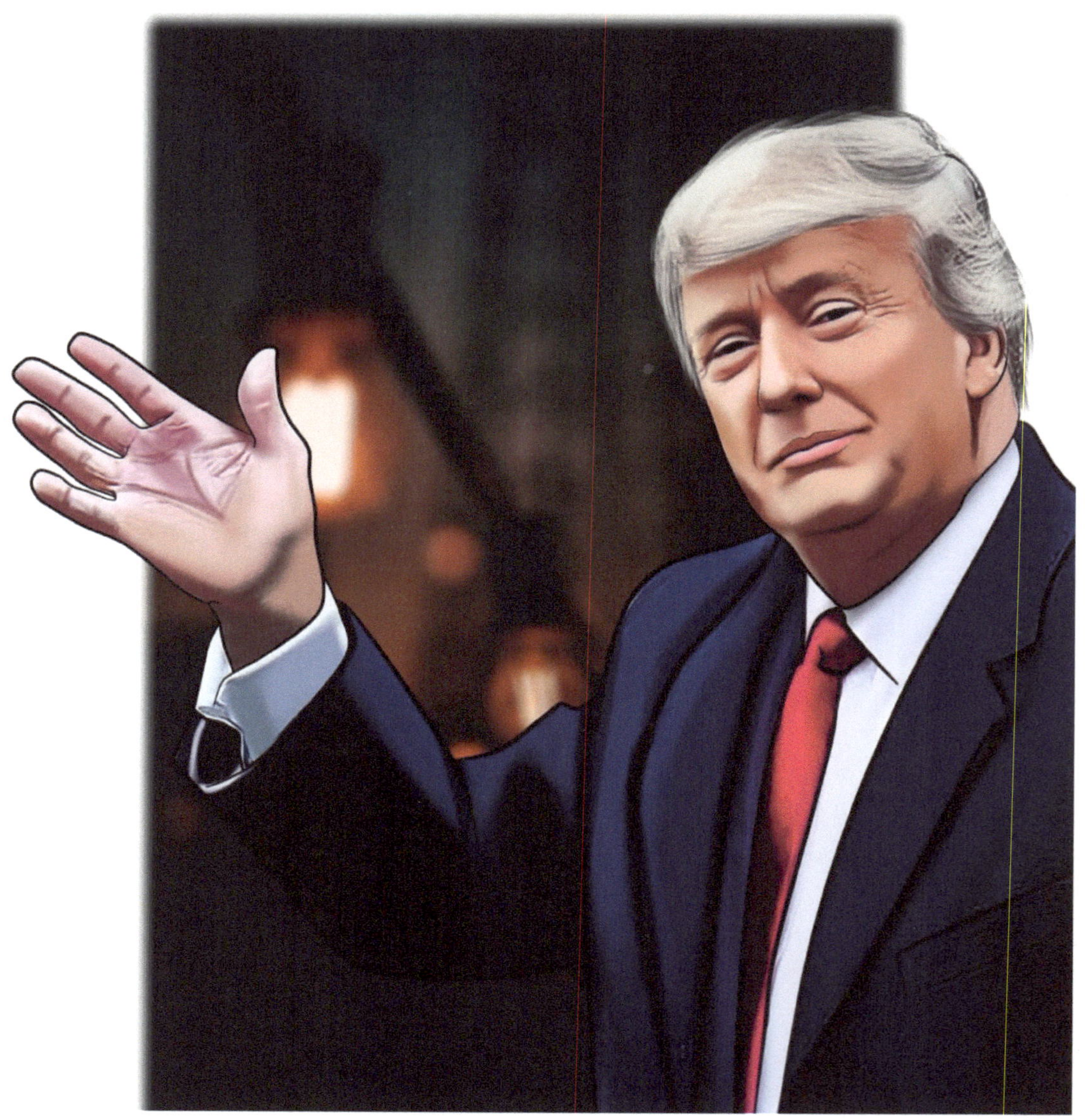

Inspired by Sarah Silbiger/Getty Images photo

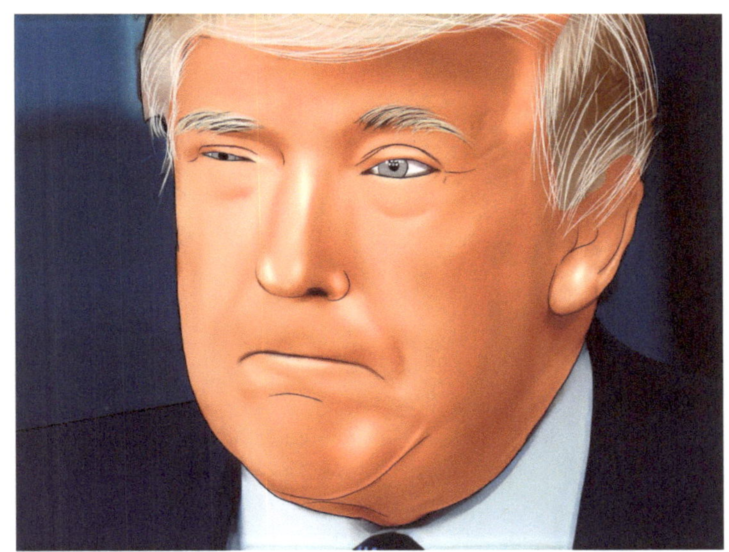

Photo inspired by screenshot of First Presidential Debate, CNN, 11/29/2020

Jun 21st 2018 - 5:51:07 PM EST

"I REALLY DON'T CARE, DO U?" written on the back of Melania's jacket, refers to the Fake News Media. Melania has learned how dishonest they are, and she truly no longer cares!

Jul 3rd 2018 - 5:19:04 AM EST

Deleted

After having written many best selling books, and somewhat priding myself on my ability to write, it should be noted that the Fake News constantly likes to ***pour*** *over my tweets looking for a mistake. I capitalize certain words only for emphasis, not b/c they should be capitalized!*

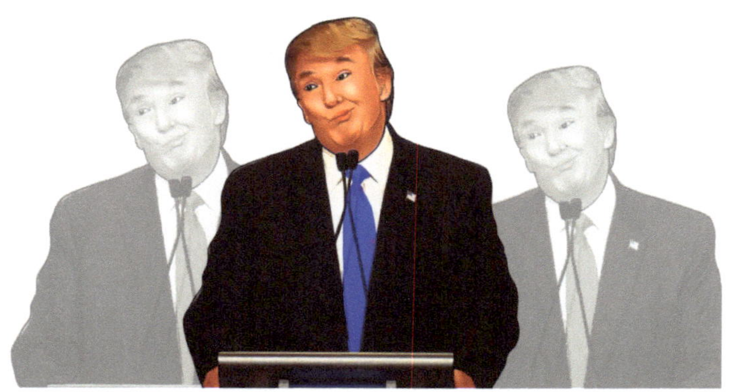

Inspired by Scott Olson/Getty Images photo

Sep 5th 2018 - 11:22:34 PM EST
I'm draining the Swamp, and the Swamp is trying to fight back. Don't worry, we will win!

Sep 30th 2018 - 12:57:45 PM EST
Like many, I don't watch Saturday Night Live (even though I past hosted it) - no longer funny, no talent or charm. It is just a political ad for the Dems. Word is that Kanye West, who put on a MAGA hat after the show (despite being told "no"), was great. He's leading the charge!

Oct 16th 2018 - 11:04:32 AM EST
"Federal Judge throws out Stormy Danials lawsuit versus Trump. Trump is entitled to full legal fees." @FoxNews Great, now I can go after Horseface and her 3rd rate lawyer in the Great State of Texas. She will confirm the letter she signed! She knows nothing about me, a total con!

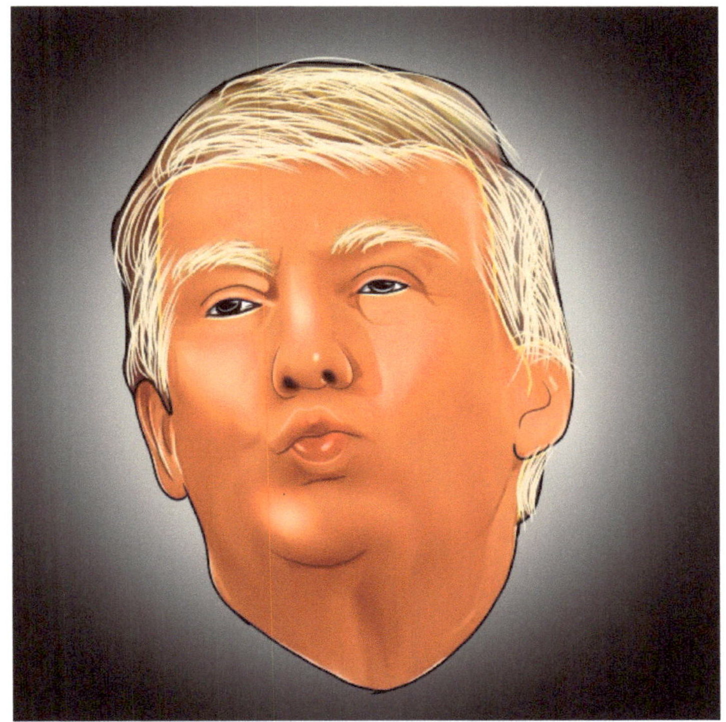

Inspired by Scott Morgan/Reuters photo

Nov 18th 2017 - 8:31:47 AM EST

Crooked Hillary Clinton is the worst (and biggest) loser of all time. She just can't stop, which is so good for the Republican Party. Hillary, get on with your life and give it another try in three years!

Jan 1st 2019 - 8:08:29 AM EST

HAPPY NEW YEAR TO EVERYONE, INCLUDING THE HATERS AND THE FAKE NEWS MEDIA!

2019 WILL BE A FANTASTIC YEAR FOR THOSE NOT SUFFERING FROM TRUMP DERANGEMENT SYNDROME. JUST CALM DOWN AND ENJOY THE RIDE, GREAT THINGS ARE HAPPENING FOR OUR COUNTRY!

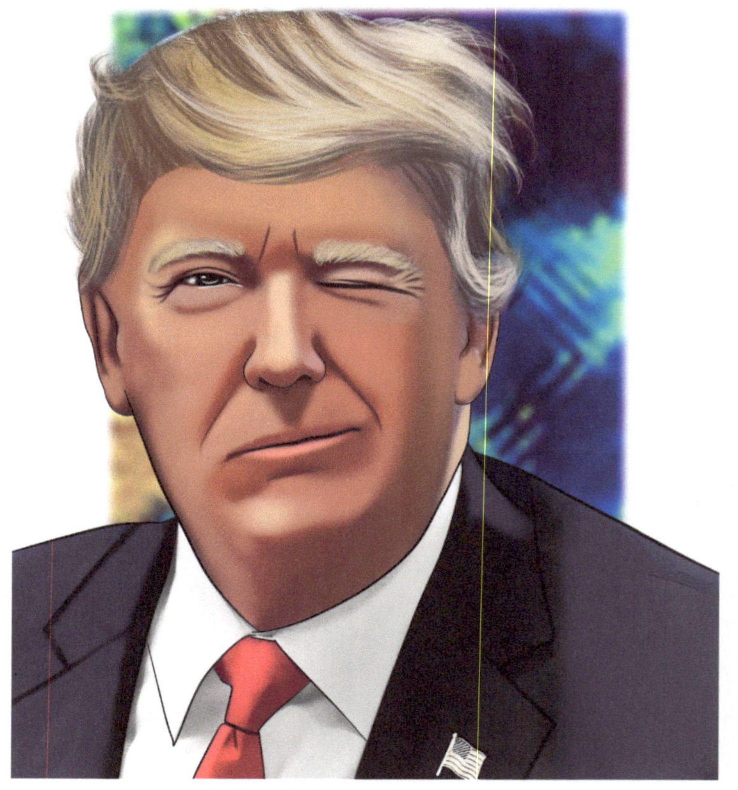

Inspired by Nicholas Kamm/Getty Images photo

Jan 4th 2019 - 8:16:20 AM EST

How do you impeach a president who has won perhaps the greatest election of all time, done nothing wrong (no Collusion with Russia, it was the Dems that Colluded), had the most successful first two years of any president, and is the most popular Republican in party history 93%?

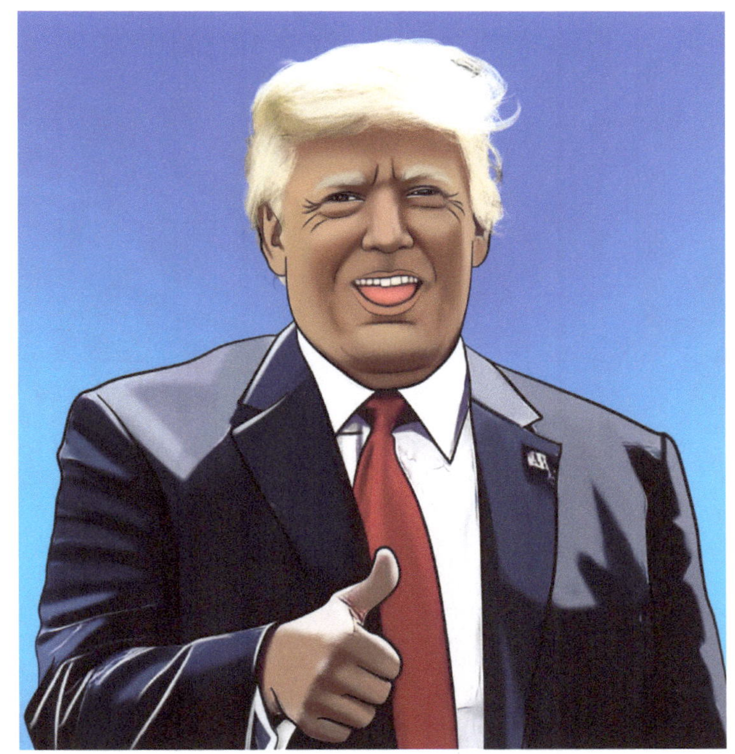

Inspired by Al Drago/Bloomberg via Getty Images photo

Jan 23rd 2019 - 2:00:06 PM EST

Even Trump Haters like (MS)NBC acknowledge you "BUILD A WALL & CRIME WILL FALL!" https://t.co/bKIgmHUW5P

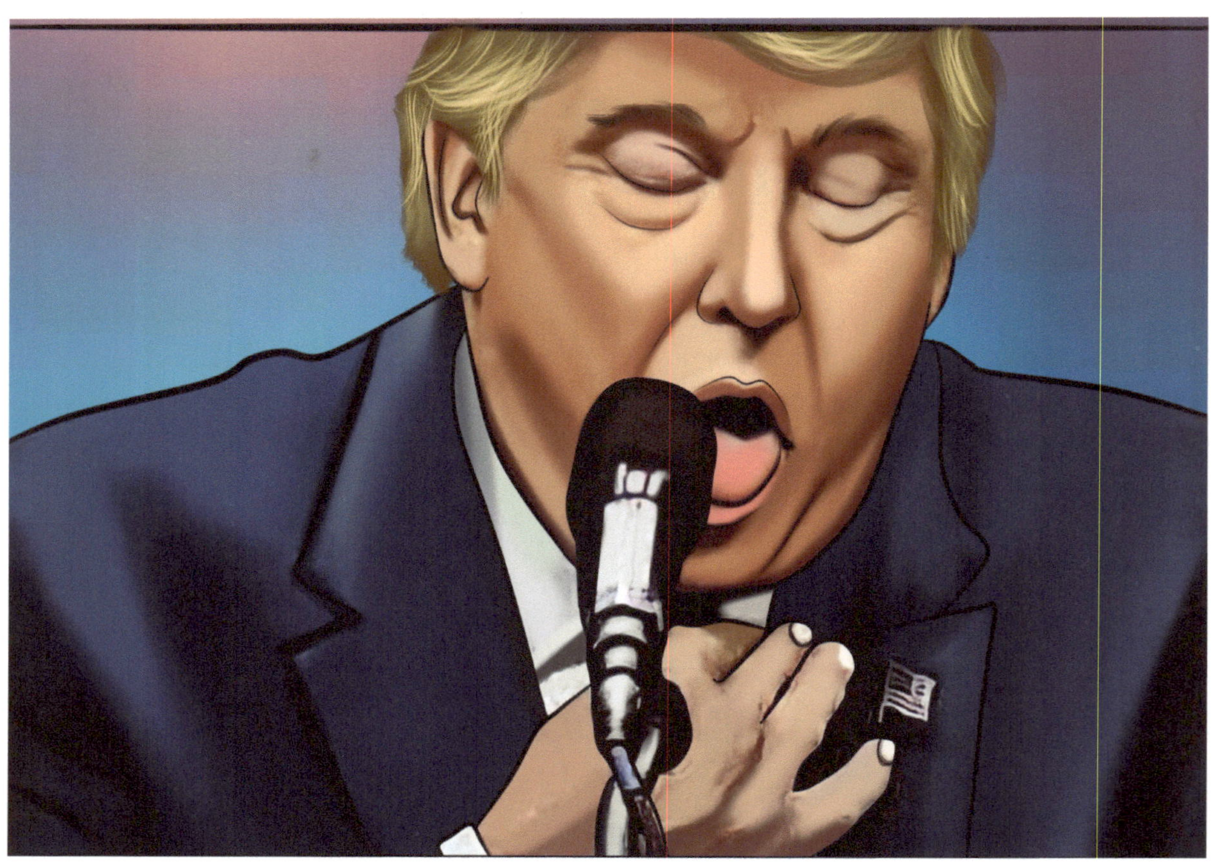

Inspired by Michael Ciaglo/Getty Images photo

Feb 17th 2019 - 7:56:09 AM EST

THE RIGGED AND CORRUPT MEDIA IS THE ENEMY OF THE PEOPLE!

Mar 19th 2019 - 9:57:04 AM EST

Facebook, Google and Twitter, not to mention the Corrupt Media, are sooo on the side of the Radical Left Democrats. But fear not, we will win anyway, just like we did before! #MAGA

Jul 24th 2019 - 3:33:51 PM EST

TRUTH IS A FORCE OF NATURE!

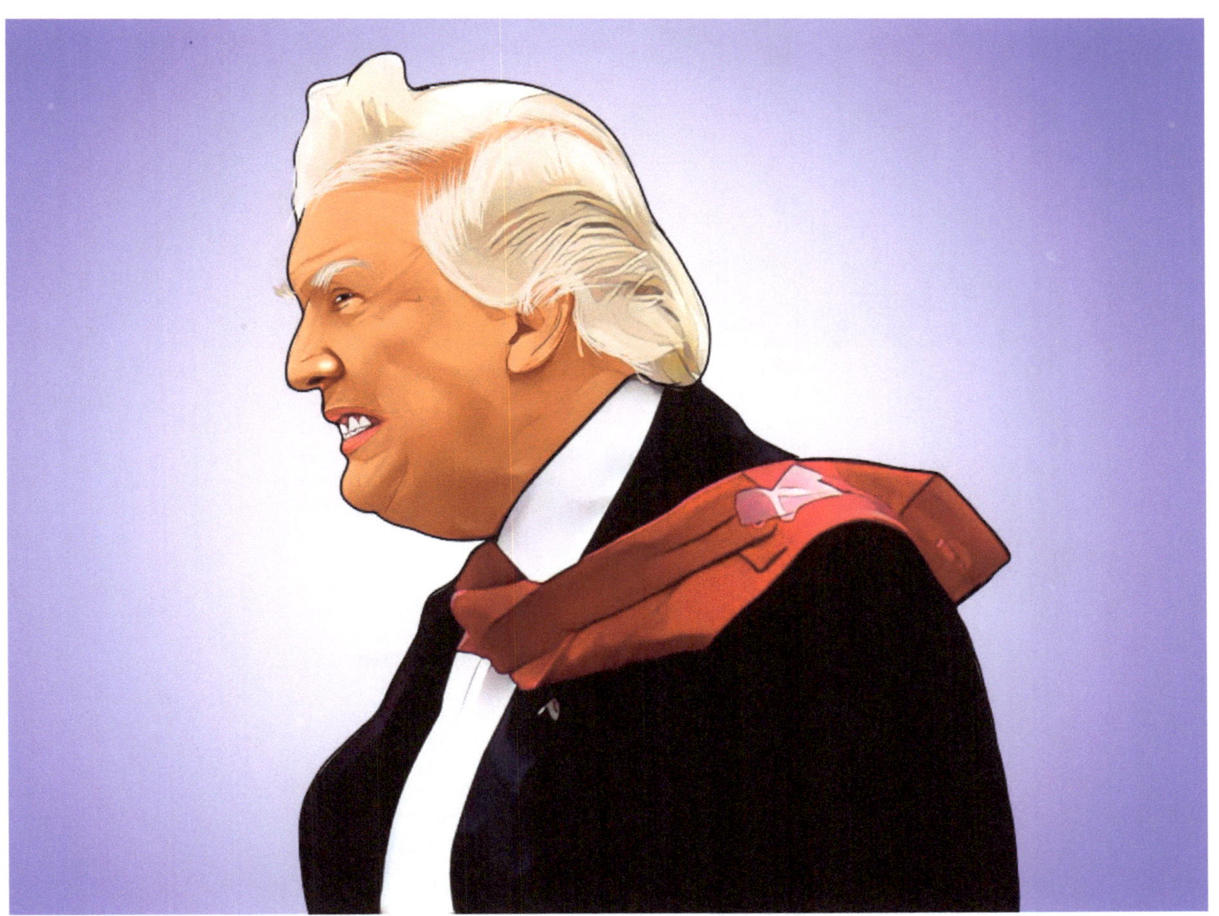

Inspired by Timothy A. Clary/AFP/Getty Images photo

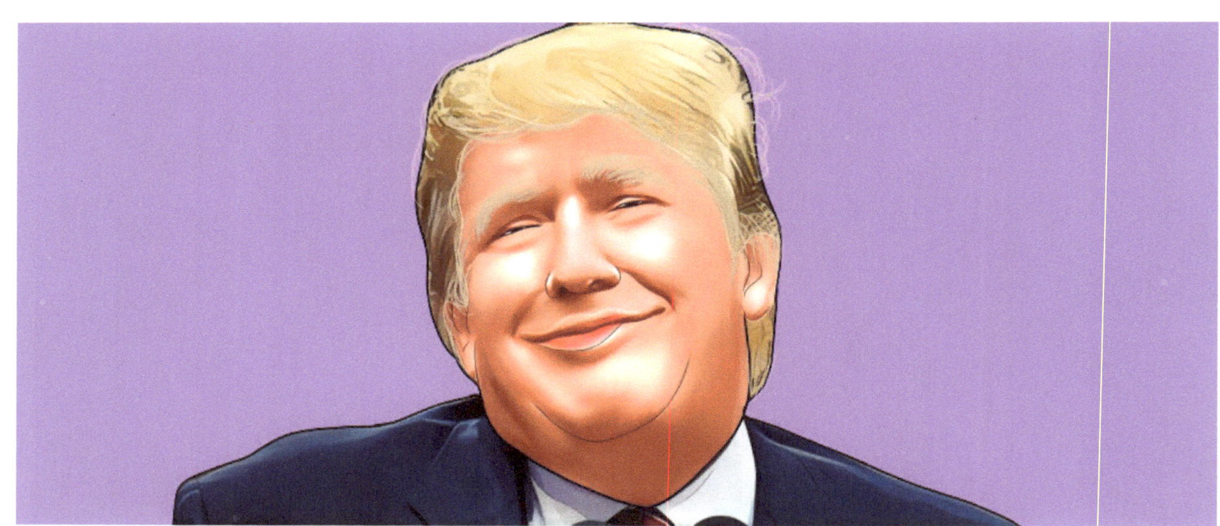

Inspired by Tom Pennington/Getty Images photo

Sep 14th 2019 - 8:44:42 AM EST

"A Very Stable Genius!" Thank you.

Sep 24th 2019 - 5:17:42 PM EST

PRESIDENTIAL HARASSMENT!

Oct 31st 2019 - 11:31:46 AM EST

The Greatest Witch Hunt In American History!

Dec 18th 2019 - 7:34:06 AM EST

Can you believe that I will be impeached today by the Radical Left, Do Nothing Democrats, AND I DID NOTHING WRONG! A terrible Thing. Read the Transcripts. This should never happen to another President again. Say a PRAYER!

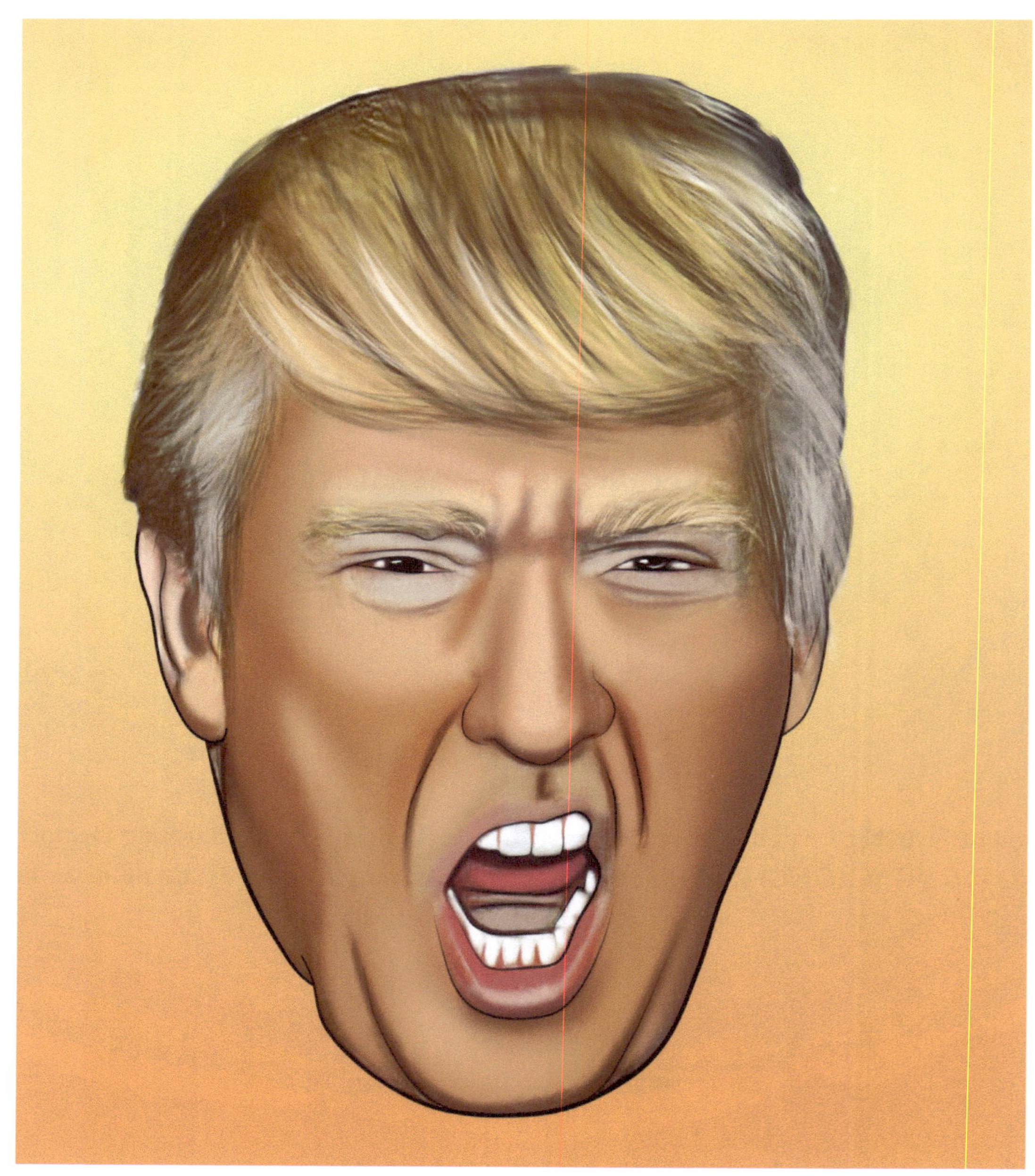

Inspired by photo sourced via https://everettcollection.com/

Jun 22nd 2020 - 7:16:57 AM EST

RIGGED 2020 ELECTION: MILLIONS OF MAIL-IN BALLOTS WILL BE PRINTED BY FOREIGN COUNTRIES, AND OTHERS. IT WILL BE THE SCANDAL OF OUR TIMES

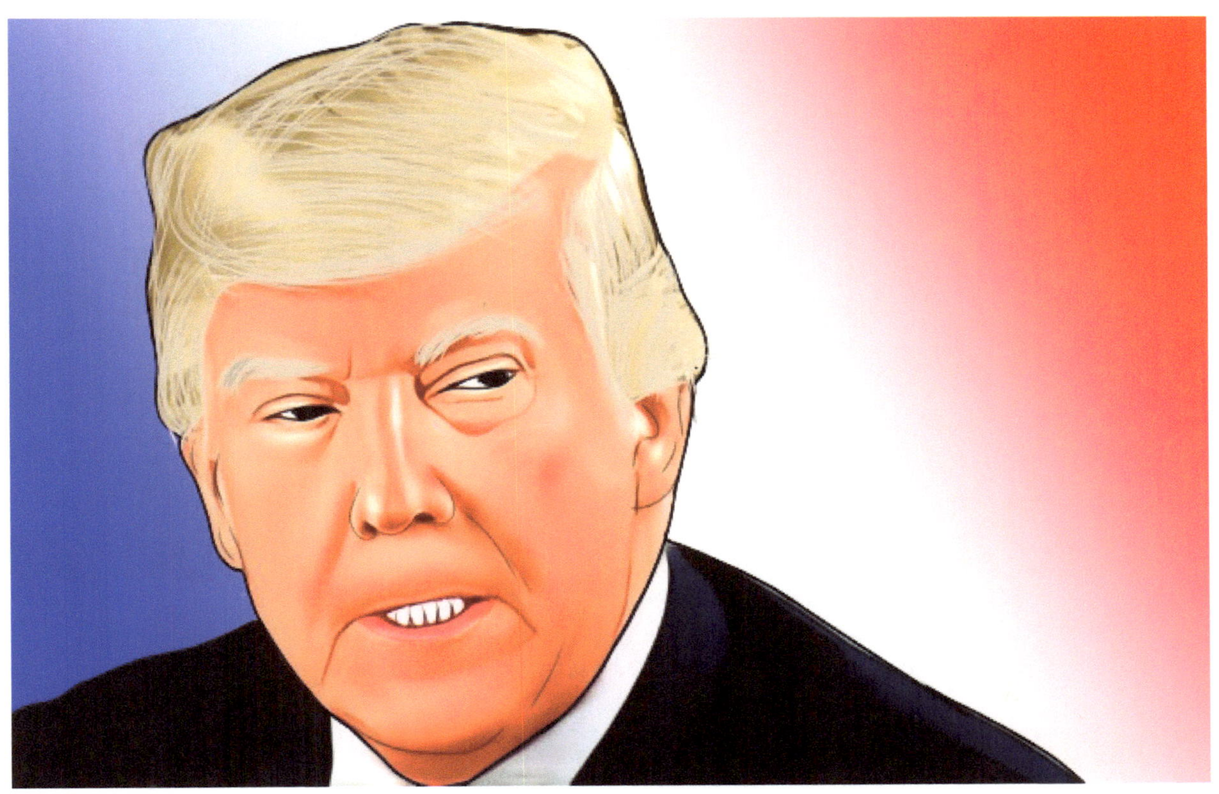

Inspired by Yves Herman/Reuters photo

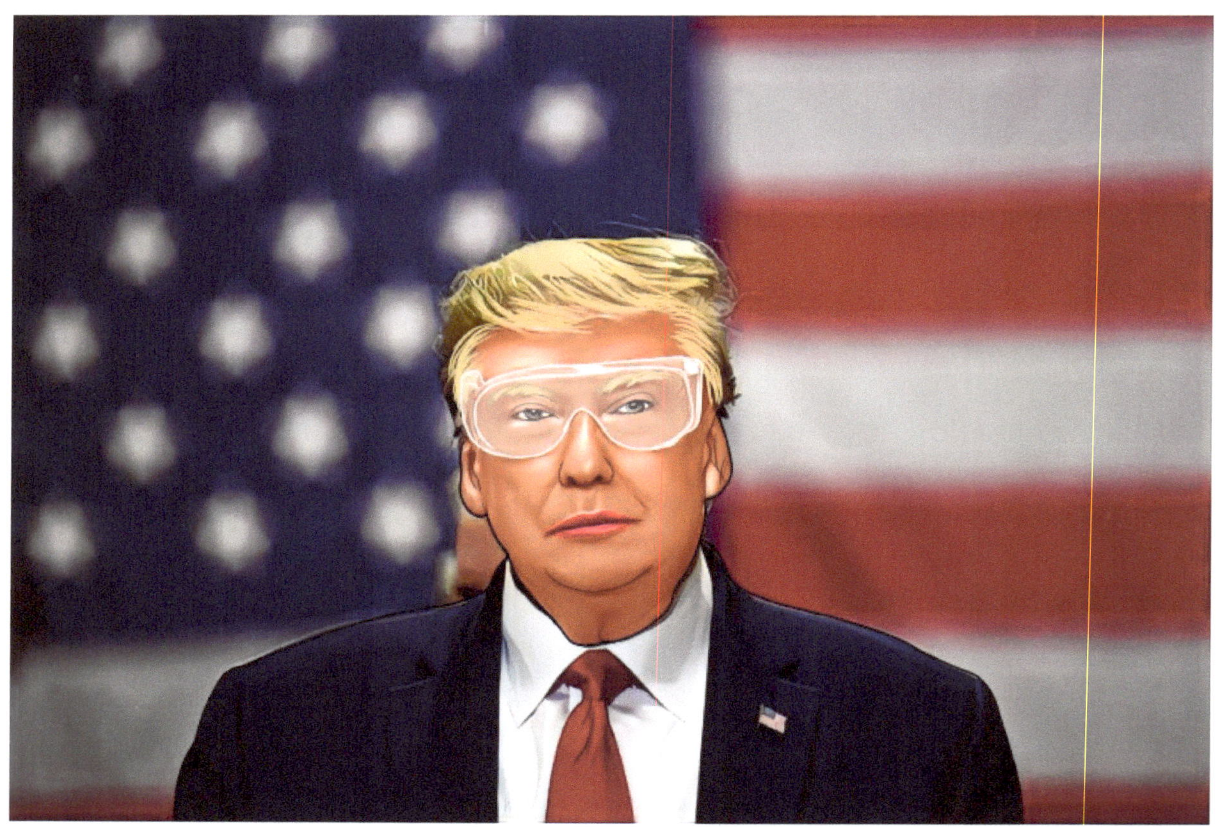

Inspired by Brendan Smialowski/AFP/Getty Images photo

Jul 7th 2020 - 10:32:07 PM EST

Deleted

Death Rate from Coronavirus is down tenfold!

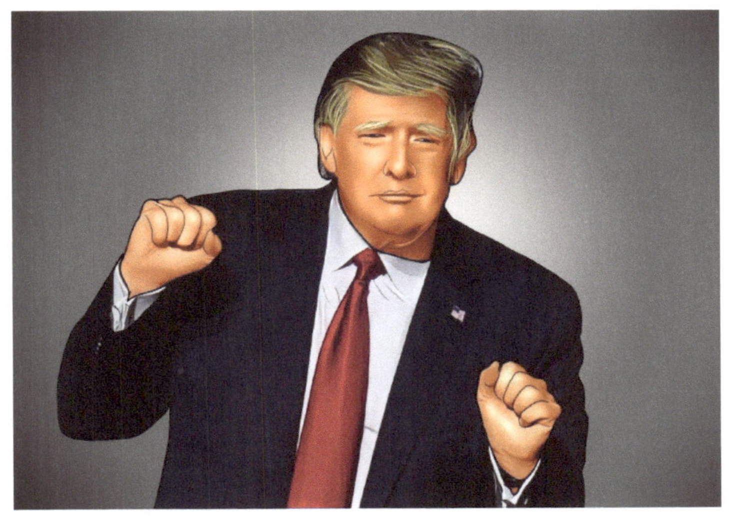

Inspired by screenshot of "Trump Dances To 'YMCA' At His Campaign Rallies" via NBC News NOW, 10/19/2020

Oct 7th 2020 - 10:51:29 AM EST

NOW THAT THE RADICAL LEFT DEMOCRATS GOT CAUGHT COLD IN THE (NON) FRIENDLY TRANSFER OF GOVERNMENT, IN FACT, THEY SPIED ON MY CAMPAIGN AND WENT FOR A COUP, WE ARE ENTITLED TO ASK THE VOTERS FOR FOUR MORE YEARS. PLEASE REMEMBER THIS WHEN YOU VOTE! https://t.co/gsFSghkmdM

Nov 1st 2020 - 6:34:06 AM EST

Our numbers are looking VERY good all over. Sleepy Joe is already beginning to pull out of certain states. The Radical Left is going down!

Nov 2nd 2020 - 1:17:14 PM EST

I PREPAID Millions of Dollars in FEDERAL INCOME TAXES!

Nov 5th 2020 - 9:12:37 AM EST

STOP THE COUNT!

Nov 7th 2020 - 10:00:27 AM EST
Deleted
Lawyer's Press Conference at Four Season's Landscaping, Philadelphia. Enjoy!

Nov 15th 2020 - 9:19:51 AM EST
He only won in the eyes of the FAKE NEWS MEDIA. I concede NOTHING! We have a long way to go. This was a RIGGED ELECTION

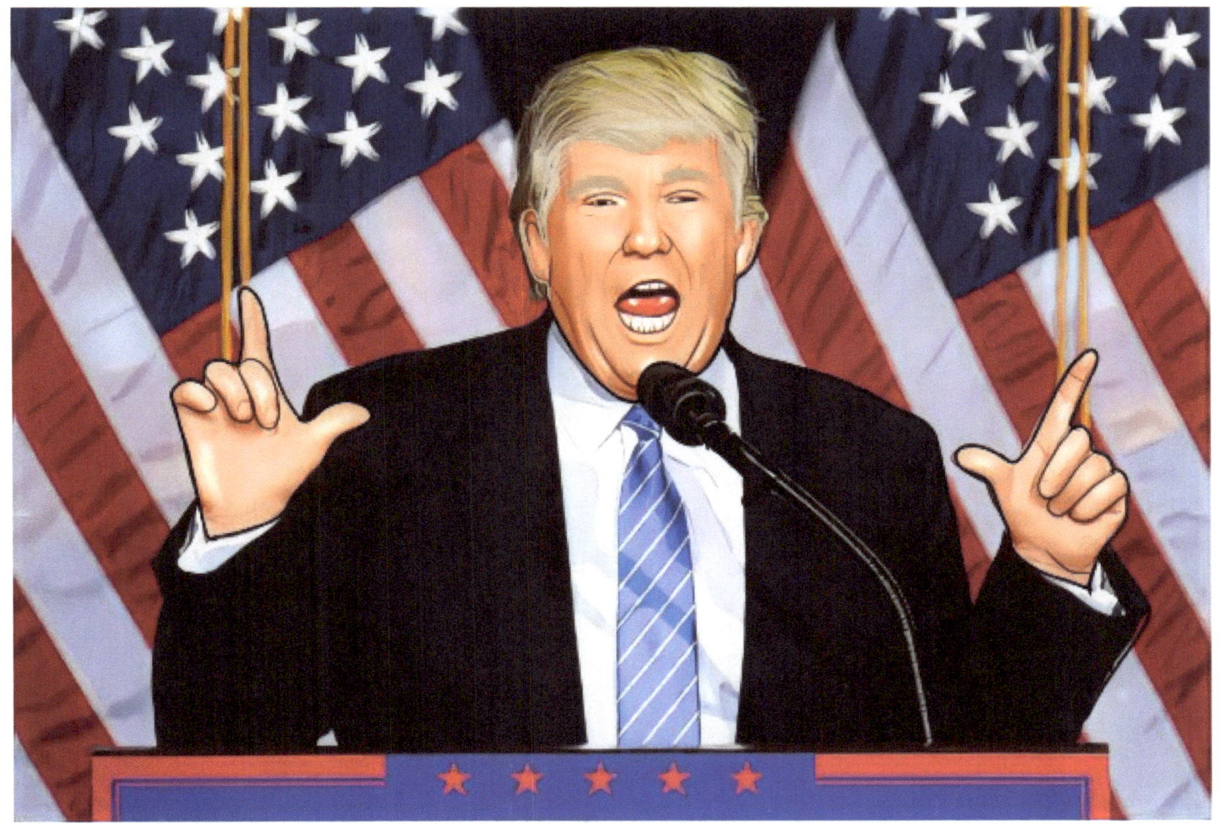

Inspired by photo sourced via https://flickr.com/photos/gageskidmore

Nov 17th 2020 - 5:40:26 PM EST

“DEAD PEOPLE VOTED” https://t.co/y6WRvCBykc

Dec 6th 2020 - 2:13:15 PM EST

...I WON THE ELECTION, BIG. https://t.co/oFF4uzNBpe

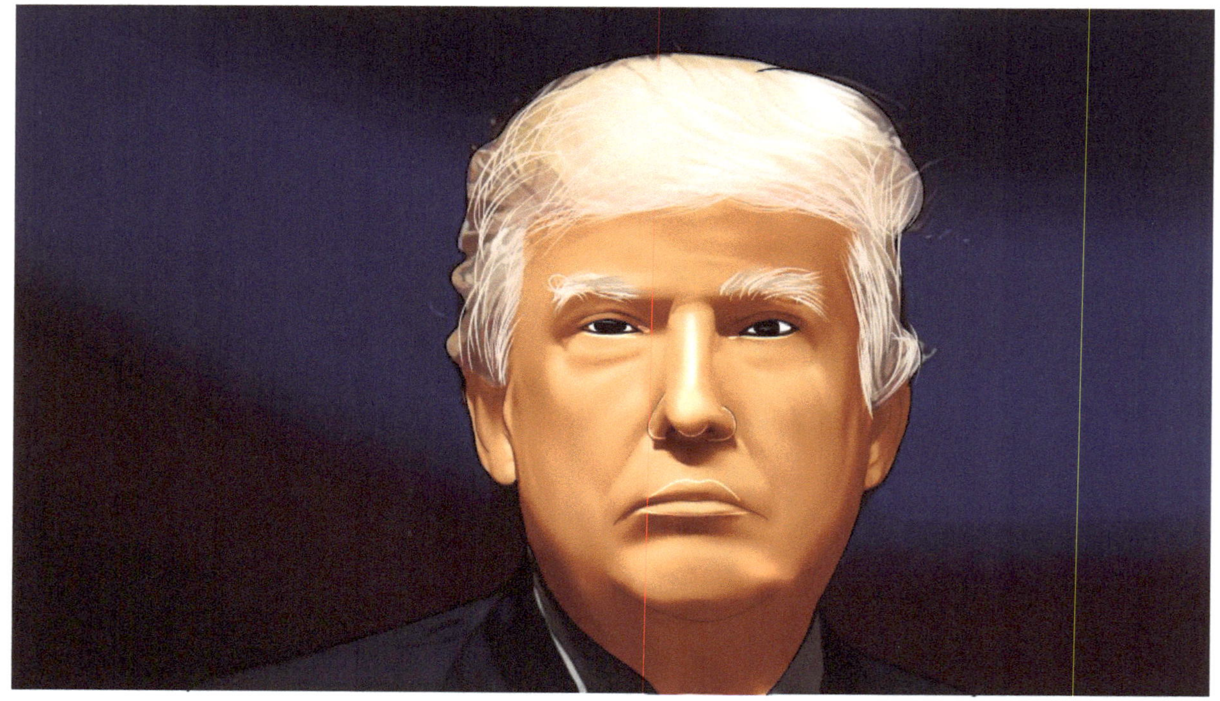

Inspired by Alex Wong/Getty Images photo

Jan 1st 2021 - 2:53:03 PM EST

The BIG Protest Rally in Washington, D.C., will take place at 11.00 A.M. on January 6th. Locational details to follow. StopTheSteal!

Jan 6th 2021 - 6:01:04 PM EST

Deleted

These are the things and events that happen when a sacred landslide election victory is so unceremoniously & viciously stripped away from great patriots who have been badly & unfairly treated for so long. Go home with love & in peace. Remember this day forever!

Jan 8th 2021 - 10:44:28 AM EST

To all of those who have asked, I will not be going to the Inauguration on January 20th.

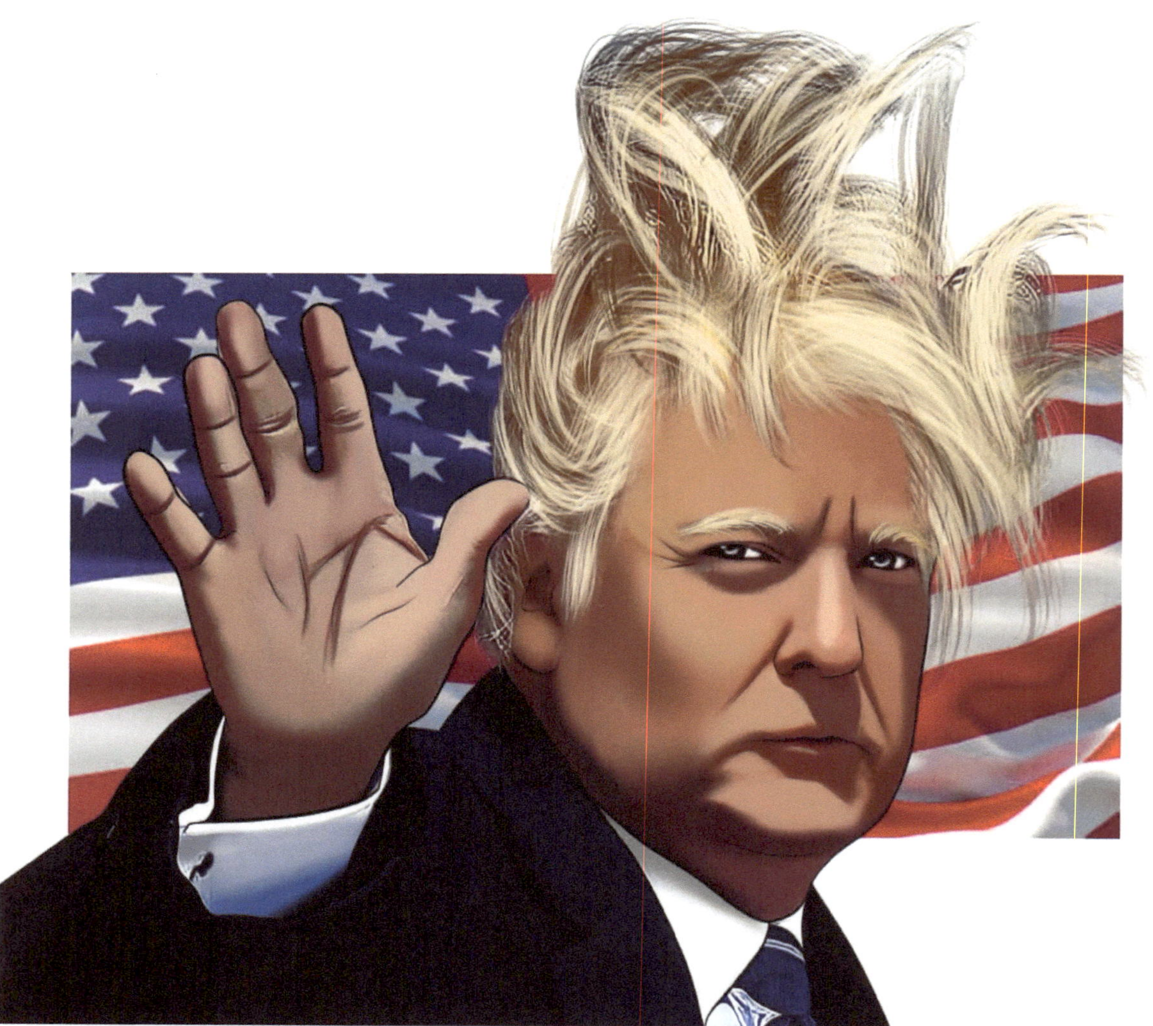

Inspired by Evan Vucci/AP photo

CPSIA information can be obtained
at www.ICGtesting.com
Printed in the USA
BVHW021221230622
640494BV00009B/402